The Four-Blocks®
Literacy Model

Writing Mini-Lessons for Kindergarten:
The Building-Blocks™ Model
by
Dorothy P. Hall
and
Elaine Williams

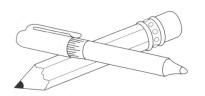

Carson-Dellosa Publishing Company, Inc.
Greensboro, North Carolina

Credits

Editor:
Joey Bland

Cover Design:
Ray Lambert

Layout Design:
Joey Bland

Artist:
Julie Kinlaw

ISBN 0-88724-119-0

Table of Contents

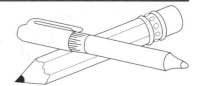

Table of Contents

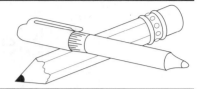

Introduction

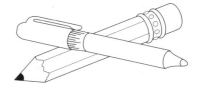

Writing is a critical part of a balanced literacy program, even in kindergarten. Some children have been read to since birth and have seen someone writing; other children have not had this exposure. In every kindergarten class, you find students who have not had many experiences with books and print. Imagine how strange the funny black marks on a page must look to these children. Have you ever looked at something written in Arabic or Chinese and wondered how anyone could ever make sense of it? To many kindergarten children, the little black marks that form English words make as little sense as characters in nonalphabetic systems make to us.

In kindergarten, the most basic concept that children must grasp is that writing is "talking written down." The black marks are not indecipherable foreign symbols. The black marks are words—the same words that people say. During morning messages, predictable charts, and writing time in Building-Blocks kindergartens, we show children what reading and writing are. We invite children to enter the abstract world of reading and writing through the very real world of their daily lives. We talk about school, the things we will do, the people we know, and the places we go. Then, we write about these same things. All children quickly learn that what we say, we can write. Soon, we invite all of our students not only to watch us write, but to become writers, writing about the things children know about and telling us all about their lives.

For many kindergarten children, writing is the easiest route to learning to read. If you observed the writing time in a kindergarten class and saw the teacher writing in front of the children and then encouraging the children in their writing, it would be natural to think that the major goal of this writing time was to teach children to write. In kindergarten and early first grade, however, another goal of the writing time is not to teach writing, but to use writing as a way to launch children into successful reading. As more children become readers by reading their own writing, the writing time then becomes a time when the major goal is to teach children how to write.

The distinction between viewing writing as a child-centered personal approach to reading and viewing writing as a way to produce better writers is critical to the success of writing time in kindergarten. If you see writing as a way to teach reading, you won't worry when you can't read what they wrote! As long as children are sitting down each day, thinking of what they want to say, and using drawing or whatever letter-sound and word skills they have to represent their ideas, you have a successful writing-approach-to-reading operating in your classroom.

If you are thinking that a writing-approach-to-reading sounds a little unusual, consider what happens with many three- and four-year-olds before they ever come to school. Have you observed young children "doing homework" like their big brothers or sisters by copying words on notebook paper? Have you noticed that the first words many young children can read are words that they can also write? Many four-year-olds have a personal reading vocabulary of important-to-them words including their names; the names of their parents, brothers, sisters, and pets; the names of their favorite restaurants; and an important phrase or two. They often write these words in all capital letters and sometimes mix up the order of some letters.

Preschool children like to draw and often add words, letters, and numbers to their drawings. Sometimes the words are written left-to-right and, for variety, right-to-left. Sometimes, the letters fit better going down the page instead of across! Children write these words by asking adults to spell them and by copying the words from print they see.

Writing and pictures by JoZanne Murphy, age 4

If you think about your family experiences with three- and four-year-old children, you will realize that combining words, letters, and numbers with drawings is a very natural activity. These "lucky" children, whose early writing efforts have been encouraged, applauded, and often displayed with pride on their refrigerators, rarely have trouble learning to read or write when they come to school. Regardless of which approach to teaching reading young children encounter later in first grade, they have already been launched successfully into reading through a very natural writing-approach-to-reading.

Writing in Building-Blocks™ Classrooms

In Building-Blocks classrooms, we read aloud to children, do shared reading with children, and provide opportunities for children to read by themselves. Similarly, we write a morning message (or a journal piece at the end of the day) for children, write predictable charts and interactive morning messages with children, and provide opportunities for children to write by themselves. We also work on phonemic awareness and letter-sound relationships or phonics, in addition to helping kindergartners learn some interesting-to-them words, as well as some high-frequency words. For more information about Building Blocks, see *Month-by-Month Reading and Writing in Kindergarten* by Hall and Cunningham (Carson-Dellosa, 1997); *The Teacher's Guide to Building Blocks™* by Hall and Williams (Carson-Dellosa, 2000); and *The Administrator's Guide to Building Blocks™* by Hall, Arens, and Loman (Carson-Dellosa, 2002).

Early in the year, the children watch each day as the teacher writes a morning message (or a journal entry at the end of the kindergarten day). The teacher thinks aloud, decides what to write, then shows the children how she would write her message. Later in the year, the writing of the morning message becomes interactive writing. The children help compose the message, spell the words, and even write the message themselves.

We also do "shared writing" of predictable charts in Building-Blocks classrooms. When writing a predictable chart, the teacher chooses the topic and begins each sentence with the same predictable pattern. Early in the year, the teacher does writing mini-lessons to show children the different ways people write and to tell children that if they cannot write (and many kindergarten children cannot write!), they can draw or "drite" (draw and write). These early kindergarten lessons let all children know that their teachers are going to accept their writing regardless.

Later in the year, the teacher begins daily writing lessons. By this time, if the teacher has written for children and with children, they know what writing is and how to think as they write. Students also know how to write words they know or listen for sounds in words they do not know and then try to represent those sounds with letters. Some teachers call these early attempts at writing the children's "developmental spelling or writing." Other teachers call it "ear spelling." We like to call it "phonics spelling." It shows us (and kindergarten teachers) what the child knows about phonics. During a brief daily mini-lesson, children observe the teacher writing and thinking about writing. Then, the children write and share their writing each day.

The writing time serves a dual function. Children who have limited literacy skills have the opportunity to use writing as an approach to learning to read. Stretching out words and listening for sounds helps some children develop phonemic awareness. As the year goes on, the children develop some reading skills as they become better writers. Writing—it does not have to be perfect writing—helps young children learn so much!

Early in Kindergarten—Getting Started

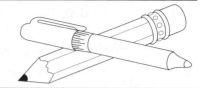

We have divided this book into two sections: Early in Kindergarten and Later in Kindergarten. Early in the year in kindergarten, Building-Blocks™ teachers focus on writing for and with children, as well as some early writing lessons to let children know that there are different ways to write. Later in the year in kindergarten, we focus on daily writing mini-lessons and provide children with an opportunity to write daily. How many lessons you do and how many times you need to revisit a mini-lesson with another example depends upon your students. This we do know—the more writing you do in kindergarten the better readers and writers you will have in kindergarten. Everything that kindergarten children write, they usually can read, too! Writing is also a wonderful mirror into each child's word knowledge.

Early in Building-Blocks kindergartens, we emphasize writing as putting down on paper what you want to tell. We write a morning message every day and predictable charts every week. Later, we do some interactive charts and interactive writing when children are ready, and most of them know something about what writing is and can use letter/sound correspondence to "write." Early in the year, we show students the different ways people write. We model driting and let children drite (draw and write). We encourage children's writing attempts. We are both coaches and cheerleaders, and we realize that at this stage of writing, kindergarten students do not need editors!

Morning Message—Showing Young Children What Writing Is

When teachers write morning messages, they provide students with models for writing. Children need to know how people think as they write and what people do when they write. As children watch and listen, they begin to understand what they are to do when asked to write. Young children learn many skills, such as swimming or riding a bike, by first watching someone else. When they are ready, they try it for themselves. This can also happen when a teacher writes a morning message. It is one of the most powerful ways to help children understand what writing is and how people think as they write. For children further along in their literacy learning, watching the teacher write a morning message can move them quickly toward independence in writing.

The morning message is usually written on a large piece of lined chart paper with a thick, black (or other dark-colored) marker. Many teachers do this activity as a part of the opening or right after the class meeting. The first morning messages are simple, using just a sentence or two.

> Dear Class,
> Today is Monday.
> We will go to music today.
> Love,
> Mrs. Hall

Each day as the teacher writes and talks about what she is writing in her morning message, she lets students know what she is writing and why she is writing it. For the first weeks, the teacher will be doing the work and the children will be listening and learning what to do and why. When the teacher finishes the message, she asks the children to count the sentences (2), count the words in the first sentence (3), count the words in the second sentence (6), count the letters in the first sentence (13), and count the letters in the second sentence (20). She counts these words and letters with the children to find the correct answers. Next, the teacher asks which sentence has more words (second), then which sentence has more letters (second). She again counts the words and letters with the children to find the correct answers. She calls on a child to answer her questions, then exclaims, "You're right! The second sentence has more words and more letters than the first!" Each day teachers do a morning message, they are showing children what writing is—but kindergarten teachers teach so much more during the morning message.

Early in the year, the teacher concentrates on saying the words and writing the letters as she says them. Some kindergartners are learning to recognize the letters of the alphabet as the teacher writes them. During the morning message, the students also learn: what you say, you can write; where to start writing and the left to right movement in writing and reading; how to say the words and letters, one at a time; how to use capital letters; how to use punctuation; how to count words; how to count letters; and how to start and end a message. The morning message stays up in the room all day and at the end of the day, the student of the day (important person of the day—whatever you call it!) takes the message home to read.

Predictable Charts—Shared Writing

Writing for children in kindergarten also includes predictable charts. For example, after spending several days learning about fall, the teacher might begin a predictable chart about fall. The teacher titles the chart "In Fall" and begins writing the first sentence, "I like to rake leaves. (Mrs. Hall)." She writes her name and puts parentheses around her name to show that the sentence is her sentence. The children add their sentences to this chart using the same (predictable) sentence starter (I like to . . . .) by telling something that they like to do in fall. After sentence dictation, which takes a day (if you have a small class) or two, the next day is spent "touch reading the sentence" or learning to track print. The fourth day is spent writing two or three sentences on sentence strips, cutting the sentences apart, then building two or three sentences. On the fifth day, children paste their cut-up sentences on large sheets of paper and illustrate their sentences. The teacher then puts these pages into a class-made big book and places the big book in the reading center for students to read and enjoy again and again. (If you have a small class and your sentence dictation only takes one day, use the extra day to read the class big book together.) Some kindergarten teachers give each child one of these books when the school year is over. Other teachers date the pages as the children write these books, take them apart at the end of the year and send a "portfolio" of their predictable sentences home so that parents can see the growth over the kindergarten year. This is a great product for the children to read during the lazy days of summer while waiting anxiously for first grade.

Early in the year, the teacher may write the sentence on the page for the child to illustrate. Later, the teacher writes the sentence, cuts it apart, and the student pastes the cut-up sentence on the page and illustrates it. As the year progresses, the student does the cutting and pasting. At the end of the year, the student may be writing, cutting, and pasting the sentence on the paper before illustrating the page. What a wonderful snapshot of a child's progress in kindergarten reading and writing. To learn more about predictable charts see *Predictable Charts: Shared Writing for Kindergarten and First Grade* by Hall and Williams (Carson-Dellosa, 2001).

Interactive Charts—Shared Reading

Interactive charts provide young children with opportunities to manipulate text and interact with print. These interactive charts also transfer oral language skills to written language. An interactive chart can be based on a nursery rhyme, a familiar poem or finger play, or theme that children are learning or have learned about. The first thing the teacher does is to write a chart and then read it to the children. The first reading (and possibly the second or third reading) are just for enjoyment. Repeated readings of the chart help young children remember the words. As emergent learners, children are active, concrete learners who need a lot of support, which interactive charts provide. The charts also help young children match oral words to written text and provide children with an opportunity to self-check and self-correct. As children read these charts and gain control over printed words, they develop an "I can read" attitude.

The steps to writing an interactive chart are quite simple:

1. Write a song, poem, or finger play on sentence strips, one sentence per strip. Four lines is an appropriate length for kindergarten. Always use your best printing so that students will see a nice, neat model for handwriting. Be aware of the size of letters, formation of letters, and spacing of your writing.

2. Place the sentences in a pocket chart, or write the chart on lined chart paper.

   Choose a part of the sentence strip for children to manipulate—a name, a rhyming word, a number word, etc. When using sentence strips and a pocket chart, the manipulated part can be placed in the pocket chart at the correct spot. (We draw a picture to go with each interactive word to help the children with the words. For the color words we put that color above each word.)

Here is an example of an interactive chart:

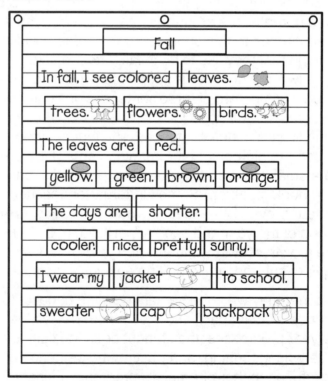

To learn more about interactive charts see *Interactive Charts: Shared Reading for Kindergarten and First Grade* by Hall and Loman (Carson-Dellosa, 2002).

Morning Message, Later—Interactive Writing

Another way for children to interact with text is to have them "help" write the morning message after the first few weeks. This shared or interactive writing is done with the teacher and students working together. They compose the morning message together, talking about it as the teacher writes it. The teacher may ask children how she should start the morning message and even how to spell "Dear" and "Class" and other familiar, high-frequency words. She may also ask children what she should write about today. Often the teacher asks questions to clarify the meaning. Sometimes the teacher lets children share the pen (or marker) and do some of the writing. (When we do this we always choose students who write legibly and who can write quickly so we do not lose children who are sitting there watching this writing.) Interactive writing starts early in the year and continues throughout the year. As the year advances, the teacher does less of the work and lets children do more and more of the composing and writing of the morning message.

The First Writing Mini-Lessons

It is best to use plain paper for the first writing lessons with your Building-Blocks kindergarten class because not all students will be ready to write on lined paper. You will have more success with students if they are familiar with morning messages (writing for children) and predictable charts (writing with children) before they are asked to write by themselves. In the first writing lessons, begin by telling the class the many ways people can and do write. Let your kindergartners know they can use pictures, lines, letters, words, pictures and words, letters and pictures, or any combination when they write. Tell students, "When you write today, use what will help you tell me something."

Early in kindergarten, emphasize writing as putting down on paper what you want to tell (we do all of our mini-lesson drawing and writing with markers). For one early mini-lesson, place a large piece of unlined paper on the board and talk as you draw a simple picture. Write a few words—labels, names, or a simple sentence. You are modeling the drawing and writing that many preschoolers do (we refer to this kind of writing as driting). Next, give the children large pieces of drawing paper and ask them to use crayons to draw and write what they want to tell you. As they draw and write, circulate around the room and "encourage" them. Respond to what they are drawing and ask them to tell you about it. Don't spell words for them but help them stretch out words and point to places in the room where they can find the correct spellings of words (names, colors, etc.). After 10 minutes of drawing and writing time, gather the children in a circle and have them "tell" what they were drawing and writing about.

Kindergartners vary greatly in their entering literacy knowledge. In some schools, many children come to kindergarten knowing how to write most letters, as well as how to read and write some words. These children have usually experienced, either at home or in prekindergarten, the writing-approach-to-reading. They know what the little black marks are, and they know that reading is just translating those marks into words they can say. They come to kindergarten already reading or pretending to read and pretending to write. For these children, writing time can soon become a time to focus primarily on learning to write better. Unfortunately, many kindergartners have not had these early writing experiences at home or in day cares, and they need longer periods of time where the emphasis is on what they want to tell and not on how well they write. In Building-Blocks kindergartens, we try to provide opportunities for all children to learn more about reading and writing.

Morning Message, Early—Showing Young Children What Writing Is All About

The first morning messages are done during the first days of kindergarten. You write for children and tell them what is happening at school that day. Early in the year, concentrate on saying the words and writing the letters as you say them. Kindergarten children are learning to recognize the letters of the alphabet as you write them. Do not ask them to sit and watch for long periods of time—just one sentence to begin with, then two sentences—five to ten minutes at the most. Share your thinking, what you are doing when you write, and why.

The teacher puts a blank piece of lined chart paper on the board and says:

"I am going to write a morning message. I will say the words as I write. Watch me. Dear, capital D-e-a-r, Class, capital C-l-a-s-s. This is a comma and the comma means to pause, stop for a second.

"I am going to write one sentence: Today, we will go to art. Today, capital T-o-d-a-y, comma, we, w-e, will, w-i-l-l, go, g-o, to, t-o, art, a-r-t." The teacher writes a period and points to the period while saying, "This is a period. You put a period at the end of a sentence.

"At the end of my message I will write the closing. I would like to say, 'I love you.' I, capital I, love, l-o-v-e, you, y-o-u, comma." The teacher points to the comma and says, "Pause; stop for a second.

"I will end the message by writing my name so that you will know that I wrote the message to you. Miss, capital M-i-s-s, Williams, capital W-i-l-l-i-a-m-s. That is how I spell my name. I have written a morning message to you. I have told you what we are going to do today."

Dear Class,
Today, we will go to art.
I love you,
Miss Williams

The teacher points to the words and asks the class to read the morning message with her.

"Let's look at the first sentence. How many words are in the first sentence?" The children join in and count the words as the teacher points to each word. "One, two, three, four, five, six."

"Now, let's count the letters in the first sentence: 1, 2, 3, 4, 5, 6, 7, 8, 9, 10, 11, 12, 13, 14, 15, 16, 17, 18." The teacher circles the capital T in Today with a marker and tells the children, "We always use a capital letter at the beginning of a sentence." The teacher then asks the children, "What else do you notice about the morning message?" She takes responses from the class and points to them in the message.

During the morning message, the children learn: what you say, you can write; where to start writing; the left to right movement in writing; how to form letters; how to use capitals and punctuation; how to count words and letters; how to start and end messages; and to talk about events at school and in the community.

The message is displayed in the front of the room all day. At the end of the day, the student of the day (or special person) takes the message home.

Other Ideas for Morning Message, Early

Be sure to write each sentence on a separate line until all children have a good concept of a sentence. Here are some other morning messages for those early weeks and ideas for many more.

Messages about the weather

Dear Class,
It is raining today.
I love you,
Miss Williams

Messages about school events, especially in the first weeks

Dear Class,
The principal will visit today.
I love you,
Miss Williams

Messages about places you visit or social studies

Dear Class,
We will go to the fire station today.
I love you,
Miss Williams

Seasonal messages (Johnny Appleseed in late September)

Dear Class,
Today is Tuesday.
We will make apple sauce today.
I love you,
Miss Williams

Messages connected to reading

Dear Class,
Today is Wednesday.
We will read "Humpty Dumpty" today.
I love you,
Miss Williams

Messages connected to math

Dear Class,
Today is Monday.
We will graph our favorite colors.
I love you,
Miss Williams

Morning Message, Later—Interactive Writing

After several weeks, the morning message becomes more interactive. The teacher asks the children questions as she writes: Where do I begin my message? What letter do I write at the beginning of that word? What do I put at the end of the sentence? What should I write next? Here is a morning message written after the first month of school.

The teacher is still talking as she writes her message each day:

"I am going to write my morning message. Dear, capital D-e-a-r, Class, capital C-l-a-s-s. This is a comma and the comma means to pause, stop for a second. I am going to write the first sentence. Tomorrow, we will go to the fair. Tomorrow, capital T-o-m-o-r-r-o-w, comma, we, w-e, will. Who can tell me what letter to write first? Yes, w; w-i-l-l, go, g-o, to . . . what letter does that start with? Yes, t; t-o, the, t-h-e, fair, f-a-i-r. What do I put at the end of my sentence?" The teacher writes a period and points to the period while saying, "This is a period. You put a period at the end of the sentence. "Now I will write the second sentence: We will see farm animals at the fair. We, w-e, will . . . how do I write will? Yes, w-i-l-l, see, s-e-e, farm . . . what letter do I write at the beginning of farm? Yes, f; f-a-r-m, animals, a-n-i-m-a-l-s. What do I put at the end of this sentence?" The teacher writes a period while saying, "You put a period at the end of the sentence."

"At the end of my message, I write the closing and say, 'I love you.' I, capital I, love, l-o-v-e, you, y-o-u, comma." The teacher points to the comma and says, "A comma means we pause; stop for a second." I will end the message by writing my name so that you will know that I wrote the message to you, Miss, capital M-i-s-s, Williams, capital W-i-l-l-i-a-m-s. That is how I spell my name. This message is about something we will do tomorrow."

> Dear Class,
> Tomorrow, we will go to the fair.
> We will see farm animals at the fair.
> I love you,
> Miss Williams

The teacher points to the words and asks the class to read the morning message with her:

"Let's look at the first sentence. How many words are in the first sentence?" She may ask a child who needs to practice this skill to count for the class as the teacher points to each word. "That's right. there are seven words. Who can count the words in the second sentence?"

One of the most powerful tools in helping kindergarten students learn high-frequency words (we call them "popcorn" words since they are always popping up in our reading and writing) and other sight words is by putting the words in the morning message each day. Students like to play word detective and find words they know in the morning message. Sometimes the teacher gives the students yellow highlighting tape and asks them to find the popcorn words and "butter" them.

Writing a morning message every day helps children learn to both read and write high-frequency words. It will pay off later in the year when you ask children to write every day.

Other Ideas for Morning Message, Later—Interactive Writing

Later in the year, wrap the sentences around, instead of putting each sentence on a separate line. Asking the class, "How many sentences?" is now a much harder task. Building-Blocks teachers never stop writing morning messages; they just let the children do more and more of the work.

Ask children what they wear when it is cold and write their responses. Talk about the three different kinds of sentences and the marks needed at the end of each. Ask children, "What letter does jacket begin with? Mitten? Hat? Can anyone spell hat?"

> Dear Class,
> It is December. It is cold outside! What do you wear to keep warm? You wear a jacket, mittens, and a hat.
> I love you,
> Miss Williams

Ask the children what they expect to see on a walk and write the answers. Again, use a variety of sentences. Ask them about beginning letters to write for some words: "What two letters do you hear at the beginning of flowers?" The following sentences have lots of high-frequency words—it, is, a, we, will, and, look, I, my, see. Ask the children how to spell the high-frequency words that keep "popping" up in your messages ("popcorn" words). Call on children who will most likely spell them correctly to tell you! When the message is finished, have someone come up and "butter" the popcorn words with yellow highlighting tape.

> Dear Class,
> It is a beautiful spring day! We will go for a walk and look for signs of spring. What do you think we will see? I hope we see lots of flowers.
> I love you,
> Miss Williams

Ask children what is going to happen this week or when important events take place. See if they can remember the plans you have made for the day. Can they tell you? Can they help you by spelling words? This late in the year, can some children help write the words you need for your message? The more they learn, the more they can help write.

> Dear Class,
> We are going to have a young authors' tea party for your parents on Friday. You will read the book you wrote! It will be a special day!
> I love you,
> Miss Williams

Predictable Charts—Shared Writing

One way to do shared writing, or writing with children, is to make a predictable chart. Predictable charts are another name for what Pat Cunningham once called "structured language experience" (Cunningham, 1979). Language experience began in the 1970s with the idea that if a teacher wrote a sentence that a student said, because it was "his" sentence, the child could read it back. This worked well for those children who came to school talking in complete sentences. For those children who did not talk in complete sentences, language experience did not work. Some children said a few words (dog and Aussie) and the teacher wrote a sentence: "My dog is Aussie." When asked to read the sentence, the child could not—it was not **his** sentence. This led to the idea of structured language experience, or predictable sentences, so all children could take part in the lesson. When making a predictable chart, all children dictate a sentence beginning with a predictable, repetitive beginning, and the teacher writes what they say. When asked to read their sentences back students usually can because of the "structure" or "predictability" of the sentences and because they know what they said to end the sentence. For more information, see *Predictable Charts: Shared Writing for Kindergarten and Early First Grade* by Hall & Williams (Carson-Dellosa, 2001).

Day 1: The teacher reads the book *ABC I Like Me* by Nancy Carlson (Viking, 1997).

She talks about all of the things she likes about herself and lets children talk about things they like about themselves. (It is okay if they are a little boastful!) Here is the start of the predictable chart "Things I Like about Me":

Things I Like about Me
I am caring. (Miss Williams)
I am kind. (Marc)
I am smart. (Susan)
I am happy. (Eleanor)
I am a good counter. (Sally)

Day 2: The teacher reads the sentences written on Day 1 and finishes the chart.

Day 3: The teacher models "touch reading" with her (the first) sentence on the predictable chart.

Then, the children "touch read" their sentences on the predictable chart. Each child reads his sentence and touches the words as he reads (tracking print).

Day 4: Sentence Builders—The teacher chooses 2-3 sentences from the chart.

She writes each sentence on a sentence strip, cuts the words apart, and gives each word in the sentence to a child. Then, she has the students with the words come to the front of the class to "build the sentence." The teacher repeats this with the second and third sentences.

Day 5: The teacher makes a class book and reads the pages in the book (or lets each child read his sentence/page.)

Other Ideas for Predictable Charts

"My Name Is" (This is an easy, must-do chart at the beginning of the year.)

My name is Mr. Bland.
My name is Joey.
My name is Suzanne.
My name is Virginia.
My name is Jennifer.

"My Favorite Color" (This is an easy, must-do chart at the beginning of the year.)

I like blue. (Mrs. Shinn)
I like pink. (Laura)
I like red. (John)
I like purple. (Mary Hannah)
I like green. (Paul)

"See What I Can Do" (This is an easy chart to do early in the year. It can also follow the reading of the book *See What I Can Do!* by Mary Pearson, Steck-Vaughn Company, 2002.)

I can write on paper. (Mrs. Murphy)
I can tie my shoes. (Zannie)
I can brush my teeth. (Joe)
I can write my name. (Marc)
I can swim in the pool. (Johnny)

"How Many People Are in Your Family?" (This is a way to review numerals or number words.)

I have 5 people. (Mrs. Costello)
I have 7 people. (Kathy)
I have 4 people. (Ray)
I have 3 people. (Christian)
I have 3 people. (Nellie)

Interactive Charts—Shared Reading

Interactive charts provide kindergarten children with opportunities to manipulate text and interact with print. An interactive chart can be based on a nursery rhyme, a familiar song or poem, or finger play. The first reading is just for the children to listen and enjoy. Repeated reading of the chart helps young children remember the words and match oral words to written text. Once young children know letters and letter sounds, it gives them opportunities to self-check and self-correct.

Getting to Know You is a familiar and popular Building-Blocks activity. Many kindergartners learn their letters and letter-sounds while learning about their classmates. Once the class has completed Getting to Know You with the children's first names, they can do the activity a second time with an interactive chart.

The teacher writes Getting to Know You statements on sentence strips, leaving enough space for student answers:

My name is _____.

I am _____ years old.

My favorite color is _____.

I like to eat _____.

I like to play _____.

The teacher also prepares the sentence strips with the answers. (She knows the answers from when the children did this orally the first time.) She writes the children's names on sentence strips for the first sentence. She writes **four**, **five**, **six**, and **seven** for the answers to the second sentence. She writes **red**, **yellow**, **blue**, **green**, **orange**, **purple**, **brown**, and **black** for the answers for the third sentence on the interactive chart. She puts the color above the word. This will help many students to be able to "read" the color words. Then, the teacher writes **pizza**, **hamburgers**, **tacos**, **grilled cheese sandwiches**, etc.—whatever most of the children said the first time around in Getting to Know You— for the fourth sentence. Once again a picture with each will help children "read" these words and select the right one. For the final sentence, the teacher writes the things most children said (for example: **football**, **soccer**, **basketball**, **video games**, **computer games**, etc.).

The teacher places the Getting to Know You statements in the pocket chart:

She places the parts the children will choose for the line after each sentence. She models one child's name and answers with that child. Then, the teacher and the class read the chart again. (Depending on the class or the child, the chart may be read a third time by the child.)

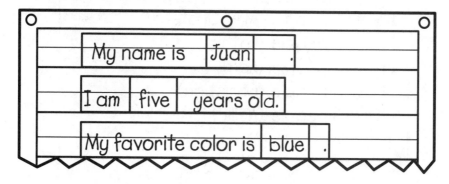

Other Ideas for Interactive Charts

Interactive Charts for Your Themes

Be sure to include words that makes sense with your climate!

Interactive Charts for Books You Read

Read *The Mitten* by Jan Brett (Putnam Publishing Group, 1996) and make an interactive chart.

Write the names of the animals; students decide which order the animals go in the mitten.

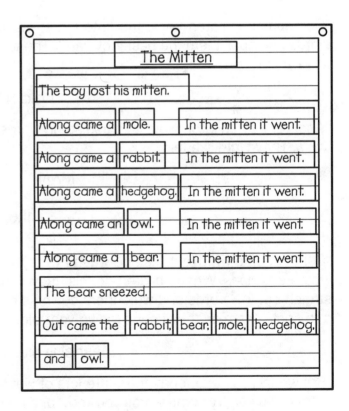

Interactive charts can be made for books you read and themes you study throughout the year.

Mini-Lesson Focus: The First Writing Mini-Lesson(s)

It is best to use plain paper for the first writing mini-lessons with your kindergartners. This way they can concentrate on writing, not handwriting. The first lesson begins with the teacher talking about the different ways people write. The lessons that follow are helpful for students who are still using pictures and random letters—they dignify those stages for all children.

The teacher talks as she draws a picture of a smiling face:

"Some children use pictures to tell stories. When I put a smile on your paper I am telling you that I like your work!

"Some children use wavy lines and call it writing. They think about what they want to say and write, 'I like school!' It looks like this:

"When children write like this they usually remember what they wanted to say. You can write like this if you want." (The teacher points to the scribbling as she says this.)

"Another way children write is to use some letters they know. They think of what they want to say and write some letters they can make. They say, 'I like pizza.' but write:

BSRB

"Sometimes children know the letters that make the sounds they want to write. They stretch out words and spell them the best they can." (The teacher stretches out, 'I played in the yard' and writes it like this:)

I pld n tha yrd.

"Another way children write is to use some words they know and some pictures for words they don't know. They write like this:

Mark ♡ hiz dog.
I like 🍕.

"Some people write just like I do when I write the morning message every day. They use words and write sentences. When children do this, they think about what they want to tell the class, then they stretch out the words and write them down as best they can." (The teacher stretches out the words and spells them as they sound to five-year-olds.)

Meshel is my frend. We like skool.

"So, when you write today there are lots of ways you can do it. You can draw, make some lines or letters, you can try some words you know and make some pictures for the words you don't know. Use what will help you to write for me."

Mini-Lesson Focus: Ways to Write—Scribbling or Random Letters

The first stage of learning to write is usually scribbling or writing random letters. Many children go through the scribbling stage at home long before they come to school. Other children have not had this opportunity, so teachers give them the opportunity and dignify this stage by modeling it. Children who have seen grown-ups write often try to write "fancy" like grown-ups do.

The teacher scribbles and talks:

"My favorite food in the cafeteria is pizza." Then, she draws a piece of pizza.

Then, the teacher says, "When I was young I thought I was writing like my mother when I wrote like this. I draw my favorite cafeteria food, pizza, here so I can remember what I said."

Some children have learned some letters and their names. When they write, they use the letters they know how to make but do not have letter-sound correspondence.

The teacher talks about a time she saw her cousin, friend, brother, etc. Then, she writes about it with random letters:

"I saw my cousin Patty last week." As she says each word, she writes a random letter.

R B M O B R C

Then, the teacher draws a picture to match her sentence.

She might add, "We had lunch together."

Then, the teacher lets the children draw pictures and write using scribbling or random letters. If some children are beyond this stage and have letter-sound correspondence, she also accepts their writing. After students draw for about 10 minutes, the teacher gathers the children in a circle and lets them show their "writing" and pictures and tell their stories.

Showing children that it is all right to scribble or write using random letters dignifies this stage of writing because some children **do** scribble and use random letters at this age, and teachers want all children's writing to be accepted. They do not want a child saying, "He's scribbling—that's not writing."

Mini-Lesson Focus: Ways to Write—Picture Writing

Some children have written before coming to school; some children have not! Depending on their experiences, some children are ready to draw, some children are ready to drite (draw and write), and other children are ready to write some words or begin to write sentences. The first writing mini-lessons should show children there are a number of ways they can write in kindergarten. By doing these lessons, children who don't know how to write words, or don't know any letters or the letter sounds, can still take part in the writing lesson and "tell" their stories.

The teacher talks about how ancient people told their stories with pictures:

"Long ago, people did not have pencils, crayons, and paper. People told their stories sitting around a fire at night. These ancient people lived in caves. Sometimes they drew pictures on the walls of their caves. These pictures were later found and now we know how cave men lived because their pictures told their stories."

The teacher draws a picture and talks about what people ate a long time ago and how they got their food. He tells the children, "People had to pick, catch, or kill their food; they didn't go into stores and buy it. How do we know? They drew pictures that are still on the walls of some caves!"

The teacher talks about how Native Americans told their stories with pictures:

"Before we lived here—before there was a country called the United States—Native Americans (sometimes called Indians) lived here. They did not have a written language. They did not have paper or anything to write with—no pencils, no pens, no crayons, or markers. They told the stories about the wars they had fought. Fathers told their sons and daughters. Children learned about their people (relatives) and their history by listening to stories. Some Native Americans drew pictures of what they did. They drew pictures of how they caught fish (sometimes with arrows, sometimes with nets) and how they killed buffaloes to make their homes (tents), clothing, and for food. Their pictures let us know how they lived and what they did; it was a way to tell stories."

The teacher asks the children to tell a story with pictures. After students draw for about 10 minutes, he gathers the children in a circle and lets them show their pictures and tell their stories.

Other Ideas for Picture Writing

Some classes need more picture writing lessons. Many young children think this is something they can do—they can tell a story with a picture. Here are some ideas:

Drawing Pictures of Family and Friends

Draw a picture of your husband, son, daughter, roommate, friend, etc., doing something they like to do and tell about it.

After drawing a simple picture, tell how Jaylen, who is just four years old, loves to go to the library and look at books, or whatever else he likes to do.

Drawing Pictures of Pets and Other Animals

Draw a picture of a pet or animal doing something that they like to do.

After drawing the picture, tell the class how your dog, Aussie, loves to dig holes in the yard! You might want to tell some ways you have tried to stop him and suggest that you also could have drawn wire fences around the bushes.

Drawing Pictures of School Activities

Draw a picture of a favorite school activity.

Tell about how the home center is fun for you to set up. Tell students you have placed some things from your home in it. . .maybe you can tell about the light your children had when they were little, your dad's old shirts, your old pocketbook, or a dish or bowl you have placed there.

Mini-Lesson Focus: Ways to Write—Copying Print in the Room

Kindergarten should be a print-rich environment. Most kindergarten classrooms have lots of print in the room for students (and teachers) to copy. For example:

- Color words
- Numbers or number words
- Month and days off the calendar
- Names on the "Name Board"
- Environmental print words (Exit)
- Print on bulletin boards
- Print from a center

The teacher models reading the room and copying some words in the room:

"I know those are the color words over there. I can see the colors and the words beside each color. I can copy those words and write any color word I want—I can even write all of them if I want. I just look around the room and copy." Show the children how you look around the room during writing—tell them that this is a good strategy to use.

The teacher writes the color words:

red	yellow
blue	green
orange	purple
brown	black
white	

He talks about drawing something in a particular color. (If you are doing this activity on chart paper or an overhead transparency, use colored pens to illustrate this.)

The teacher writes a name from his "Name Board" or "Name Wall" and draws a picture of that person.

The teacher models "writing-the-room," by using a clip board, pencil, and plain paper to write some more words from around the room.

He encourages children to copy some print in the room and illustrate that print.

After students write and draw for about 10 minutes, the teacher gathers the children in a circle and lets them show their writing and illustrations.

Mini-Lesson Focus: Ways to Write—Sounding Out Words

Some children know the letter names and the sounds those letters make but do not know how to use that information when they are writing. To help those children use what they know when writing, sound out a word to model "phonics spelling" for children. If they do not know any letter names or sounds made by letters, you can still model this and let the kindergarten children try, remembering to "ooh" and "aah" over their attempts.

The teacher writes some sentences by stretching out words:

She is sure to choose some "big" words that are not in the children's reading or writing vocabularies so all children will have to stretch out the words and watch her write the letters.

Miss Williams's mother is Greek and likes to eat spanokopita. (span-o-ko-pit-a)

I would like to go to Hawye. (Ha-wy-e)

My friend wants to go to Australya. (Au-stral-ya)

The teacher encourages the children to write something, str-e-t-ch-ing out the words and writing the sounds they hear. After students write and draw for about 10 minutes, she gathers the children in a circle and lets them show their pictures and "read" their phonics spelling stories.

Mini-Lesson Focus: Drawing and Writing (Driting)

Early in kindergarten, you need to make it okay for children to write in whatever way they can. Children need to get in the habit of "telling something" when they write, and some children become comfortable using pictures, words, and combinations of pictures and words. We model this in our early-in-the-year mini-lessons by drawing something and just writing labels or a few words to go with our pictures. Here is an early-in-the-year driting lesson.

The teacher puts a blank piece of unlined paper on the board (or a transparency on the overhead) and says:

"Today, I am going to draw and write to show you what I want to tell you about."

The teacher talks about her family as she draws them:

"Here I am. I am wearing my Wake Forest T-shirt and getting ready to watch the Wake Forest football game on television."

"I will write my name under my picture, and I will write TV under the picture of the TV."

The teacher writes Miss Williams and TV under the appropriate pictures.

"Sometimes when we write, we use pictures and words to tell the story. Today, I wanted to tell you about my favorite college team. I cheer for Wake Forest to win when they play football or basketball on television. I used pictures to show me and my television. I used letters on my shirt to show the team I cheer for. I used words to write my name. I know that many people say TV for television, and I know how to make those letters, so I write TV under the TV or television."

"Now, I want you to draw and write something you want to tell me. You can draw and write about you or your family, or you can draw and write about anything else you want to tell. If you draw and write about you, your pictures and words will be different from mine because you look different and have a different name."

The teacher gives the children unlined paper and encourages whatever level of drawing and writing they can do. After 10-15 minutes, she gathers them in a circle and lets them tell her about their driting.

Other Ideas for Drawing and Writing (Driting)

Driting is an easy entry into writing. Depending on your children, do as many driting mini-lessons as they need to all feel that they can write.

Drawing and Writing about Pets

Most children are interested in pets. Draw and write about pets you have, or pets you had when you were a child, or pets of a relative or friend. As you draw, tell lots of details. Write a label or two to go with your drawing.

"When I was little, I had a dog named Spot. He was a little spotted dog. He was a quiet, friendly dog and did not bark a lot. He liked for me to take him for a walk.

"I am going to write the words Spot under the picture of the dog and Miss Williams under the picture of me when I was little."

Remind children that they should draw and write what they want to tell you. They might write about a pet, but they might write about something entirely different.

Drawing and Writing about Vehicles

Children are always interested in things that go—bikes, scooters, buses, cars, trucks, etc.

"I drive my car to school, but on the weekends I like to walk and ride my bike. I walk to my mom's house. Sometimes I ride my bike around the neighborhood or to the store. Walking and riding my bike are fun and good exercise."

Draw a bike and under the bike write green bike—point at the color words in your room and tell the children how you found it on the color chart and copied it. Then, draw yourself as best you can. (Five-years-olds think we can draw well.) Beside your picture, write your name.

Other Kid-Appealing Topics for Driting

Here are some other ideas for drawing and writing about in kindergarten:

- favorite foods (pizza, apples, tacos, etc.)
- places (mall, grocery store, park, lake, etc.)
- relatives (grandma, cousin, baby sister, etc.)
- friends
- movies
- sports

Later in Kindergarten—Getting Better

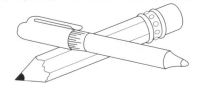

Once five-year-olds know what writing is and how people write, they are ready to write on their own. Teachers who set aside time every day for their kindergarten classes to write develop both good readers and good writers. We have found that doing a brief mini-lesson before the children write helps move all children forward in their writing. In our daily writing mini-lesson, we think aloud about the things we could "tell them." We make a list on the chalkboard, a piece of chart paper, or on an overhead transparency. We tell our stories by drawing and writing a few words during our first mini-lessons. Later in the year, the writing in these mini-lessons becomes a sentence or two each day. After we write, we ask the children to write. As the children write, we circulate around the room and "encourage" them. We don't spell words for them, but we help them stretch out words, and we point to places in the room where they can find the correct spelling of words. After 10-15 minutes of drawing and writing time, we gather the children in a circle and have them "tell" what they were drawing and writing about. We always ask young children to "tell" about their writing. This makes it possible for all children to take part in this activity. If we ask them to "read" their writing, some children may say they can't read it, but everyone can tell us what they wrote about.

Here are some of the signs we look for to let us know we can move on and put a greater emphasis on helping children to focus on becoming better writers. Most days, most children:

- seem comfortable using words and pictures to put down what they want to tell.

- use print displays in the room to spell words.

- stretch out words not available in the room, getting down enough letters so that most words are decipherable.

- can write one or more sentences that they can read back to us.

- during the daily circle time, can tell about what they have drawn and written.

Once most children display these behaviors most of the time, we can move on. Now, we show students how they can take several days to write about something if they need to. We start writing about something one day and finish it by "telling more" the next day. As the kindergarten year continues, the writing time begins to look more like a Writer's Workshop and more like it does at other grade levels.

Most kindergarten teachers allow some time after writing for children to share their work, usually in a circle-and-share format. In some classrooms, Author's Chair procedures are established and some of the children are chosen to share each day instead of circle-and-share. Each teacher must decide what works best for his class. The important thing is for the children to have more of an audience than just the teacher.

What the children write about usually changes, too. Early in the year, children have been drawing and writing on unlined drawing paper. Whatever subject the teacher models is usually the subject chosen by most children. As teachers encourage children to add to the sentences and the writing is extended over several days, then the children usually start writing more on topics they choose rather than on the teacher's model. Building-Blocks teachers usually do not let children copy their writing. Teachers tell students, "This story is about **my** cat, you can tell about **your** cat, dog, hamster, etc." Or teachers say, "This is about **my** trip to the mall; now you tell about **your** trip to the mall, grocery store, gas station, etc." Building-Blocks teachers also do not write for children. If teachers write words under the child's writing to remember what the child "wrote," the child perceives that her writing is not real or good. A good strategy to try is writing in cursive on small self-stick notes and attaching them to the backs of the pages. This helps teachers remember the text at a later date without discouraging young authors. However, if a child does not know letter sounds, then the teacher would encourage him to draw or copy print in the room.

Most of the year, a drawing is usually included with the daily writing. Some children like to draw first and then write about their drawing. Other children like to write first and then illustrate their writing. Kindergarten children like pictures to go with their writing—just like the books that are read to them!

Most kindergarten teachers use writing notebooks or "journals" for the children to write in. The children keep their daily writing in these journals. Beginning in January, some teachers (including Elaine) like to staple 20 pieces of paper together with a front and back cover, write "January Journal" in their best printing and let the children use these each day to write in. Many times, Elaine has wrapped these blank journals in holiday paper and ribbon and given them to the students as a holiday gift in December, letting the children know that they will start their daily writing as soon as they return from the holidays.

In Building-Blocks™ classrooms, teachers help children learn how to write, but teachers do not edit kindergarten writing. They leave that for first grade! Kindergarten teachers just celebrate what they can do each day when writing and help each child get better by coaching them one-on-one. For most of kindergarten, Building-Blocks teachers encourage the children to write about whatever topics they choose in whatever form they choose. During the last months of school, kindergarten teachers look at each child's writing and choose a piece to publish (or make public). Each child makes a book and reads it at the Young Author's Conference or Tea during the last weeks of school. Some kindergarten children write quite well, and teachers just have to copy (or type) their pieces over. Other children need coaching from teachers as they write, encouragement to illustrate the sentences on each page, and finally someone to listen to them practice reading their pieces several times.

In order to get a book published for each child in the class, you may have to look for more time. You may find time to coach during writing time and also at center time. You can put a sentence on each page. Sentence by sentence type a child's "story," cut the sentences apart, paste each sentence on a page of a premade book (eight half-pages of paper and covers stapled or put together with a bookbinder), and have the children read and illustrate each page. Sometimes a child's book is already typed on the class computer and you just have to cut the sentences apart. Sometimes you can compile the children's writing on one topic (spring, mothers, kindergarten, summer, a field trip, etc.) into a class book and duplicate it so each child has a copy to take home. Having individual class books or student-authored books gives kindergarten children a souvenir of kindergarten and something to show to relatives and friends.

Mini-Lessons

Doing a good mini-lesson every day helps young children learn to write. You can tell them what to do over and over again, but like the old saying, "A picture is worth a thousand words!" We have found this to be especially true about writing—showing is far more powerful than telling. The mini-lesson is your chance to show children how to do all of the different things writers do when they write. We keep the mini-lesson brief, 3-5 minutes as we begin, and write a sentence or two every day for the children. We model stretching out words and hearing the beginning, middle, and ending sounds. Sometimes students give the letter sounds they hear as we write them down. We also talk about capitalization and punctuation we will use. We usually focus on one skill or strategy that we need to teach or reteach to our young students. As we write, and before and after writing, we "think-aloud" about what we are doing. This allows the children to see how we make all of the decisions a writer must make.

We think aloud about what to write and how to write it:

"Let's see. What do I want to tell you today? I could tell you about what I did after school yesterday—or I could tell you about my new neighbors who moved next door. I know! I will tell you about the birdbath I put in my front yard last weekend and how the birds visit and bathe in the water."

We think-aloud about our spelling strategies:

- "I want to say, 'A red bird came to my new birdbath yesterday.' I can look over there on the wall and see all the color words. I can use these to find and spell red because a red bird came to my birdbath."

- "I can see the word bird up on the "Spring" bulletin board. I'll look there and copy it."

- "I want to write **came** next, so I will stretch it out and write the sounds I hear ('c-a-m') I know how to spell **to** since I write it all the time in my morning message. I also know how to write **my**. I want to write **birdbath** so I look at the word **bird** I wrote, write it again, and add **bath** (stretch it out and spell it.)"

We think aloud about punctuation and capital letters:

"I know how to write the word **a**. Since it is the first word, I know to start my sentence with a capital letter. This is the end of my sentence, so I will put a period. I start my next sentence with a capital T."

We think aloud about adding on:

"This is the piece I began yesterday, but I didn't finish it. I will reread what I wrote yesterday to get my brain thinking again. . . . Now I am going to tell you what the birds do when they get wet. 'They flap their wings to dry them off. . . .'"

We keep showing kindergarten children how to write.

We do not expect everyone will write as we do, so we remind the children about drawing and writing letters, and stretching out words and putting down sounds as we do the lessons at this time of year.

We do many different mini-lessons focusing on the same writing strategy so that children will get the idea from repeated lessons. Five-year-olds don't learn everything the first time teachers tell them. We return to strategies we previously taught when we observe something in the children's writing they particularly need to focus on.

Once we start to publish, we do a mini-lesson on how to turn an unedited piece into a published book. Children watch us carefully copying or typing the pages, cutting the text apart, illustrating each page, and assembling the book. We talk about how the pictures have to match what it says on the page. (We might reinforce this during our read-aloud when we show how these pictures match the text on each page.) In kindergarten, publishing takes time, help, and patience, but it pays off as the children really begin to see themselves as writers.

Because it is impossible to know how many mini-lessons you will need for each focus, we have included one full mini-lesson and then lots of ideas for other lessons. These other lessons can be done right after the first one or you can return to a mini-lesson focus weeks later when observations of your children's writing let you know that they need review and reteaching.

As children begin to write, we provide one-on-one help to our most capable students. Once they are independent (and that does not take long), we go on to our average students, then struggling children. Kindergarten students do not really need coaching while they are scribbling and drawing the way they do when they know the letter sounds and are ready to stretch out words and write the sounds they hear. When coaching, we ask the children to whisper their sentences to us, or we ask them what they want to tell and help them construct simple sentences. Then, we help them stretch out the words in those sentences and point them to words on the word wall and on other print displays. We help them put a finger space between words, and we ask them to read their sentences back to us, pointing to each word as they read. This daily, individual coaching of students, especially the most struggling writers, makes a remarkable difference in their abilities to write sentences that they can read and talk about.

We also pay attention to our advanced writers, reading with them what they have written. We marvel at how well they used the print resources in the room, stretched out words, and wrote three (or whatever number) whole sentences! With your help, each child can write a sentence, and the paper has plenty of room for three or four sentences. When you gather the children in a circle for sharing, be sure to comment on all of the interesting things they told and their spectacular drawings (much better than yours!), as well as how much and how well they have written. They will all feel successful if you brag on their ideas, drawing, and writing!

The following section of this book contains mini-lessons we do later in the year in kindergarten. We do as many of each as our particular class needs. We come back to lessons done earlier if we notice children who need to review that strategy. If you notice something that children need to focus on that is not covered in these mini-lessons, create mini-lessons of your own using the lessons outlined here as models.

Over the years, we have observed that teachers who have the most successful writers in their classrooms faithfully do a mini-lesson every day in which they model and think aloud about every aspect of the writing process. In fact, we have concluded that the quality, variety, and explicitness of the mini-lessons usually distinguish teachers who enjoy teaching writing from those who don't. In this book, we have tried to capture the spirit and essence of all of the excellent kindergarten mini-lessons we have seen and share them so that you and your children can feel happier and be more successful with writing. The most important thing to remember is to let your kindergarten students write every day. Do not look for perfection, look at writing as a daily opportunity for students to pull up and show you what they know about phonics and written language. Celebrate the little things that they know and do. Brag on letter-sound correspondence. Five-year-olds are not great spellers, but when they do the work and know the letter names and their sounds, we can read their "phonics spelling." Most of all, have fun—we do when we write with kindergartners!

Mini-Lesson Focus: Modeling How to Write a Sentence

Writing a good, complete sentence is not an easy skill to learn in kindergarten. Children need to learn to write good sentences and there is really no way to explain what a good sentence is at this grade level. The best way to help all of your children learn how to write good sentences is to do some early mini-lessons in which you only write one sentence and you talk with the children about the sentence. A good sentence makes sense to the person who is hearing or reading it, and because it makes sense, we can draw it.

The teacher draws and thinks aloud:

"Here is my car. I am driving to Greensboro where my sister lives. I love to go and visit my sister, Laura, and her three children."

The teacher writes:

I like to visit my sister.

The teacher asks:

"Who is this sentence about?"

"Where did I go?"

"Who did I visit?"

"Yes, this is a sentence about me. It tells where I went. I went to Greensboro. Who did I go to see? Yes, I went to visit my sister who lives there."

The teacher tells her students that she is going to walk around as they begin drawing their pictures.

She wants each student to whisper to her the sentence he is going to write today before he writes it. If a child says one complete sentence, she tells him that it is a wonderful sentence and moves on to the next child. If a child doesn't tell her a complete sentence, she helps him say a complete sentence before the child writes. If a child tells her several sentences, she tells the child that he has three (or whatever number) good sentences and helps him find the end of each sentence as he says it.

After the children write, the teacher gathers the students in a circle and lets them share their pictures and sentences.

Other Ideas for Modeling How to Write a Sentence

Doing More "Draw and Write One Sentence" Mini-Lessons as Needed

Draw a picture of a pet and write a sentence about that pet.

This is my cat, Butch Kitty.

Talk about your pet and read your sentence. Ask, "What kind of pet do I have? What is my cat's name?" Circulate as children begin to draw and write and have them whisper their sentences to you before they write. Help each child write a sentence and illustrate it. Finally, gather the children in a circle and have them share their pictures and sentences.

Drawing a Picture and Letting Children Help You Come Up with a Sentence

Draw a picture of you doing something you like to do. Ask your class to help you come up with a good sentence to go with your picture.

Mrs. Hall likes to read books.

Circulate as your children begin to draw and write about the things they like to do. Have the children whisper their sentences to you before they write. Help them to form good sentences and illustrate them. Finally, gather the children in a circle and have them share their pictures and sentences.

Rereading a Book with One Sentence per Page and Writing a One-Sentence Response

Show children a book you have recently read to them that has just one sentence on each page. Reread a few pages from the book and help children notice that each page has a picture and one good sentence. For the writing part of your mini-lesson, write one good sentence that summarizes the book. If the book you reread was *Curious George Takes a Job* by H.A. Rey (Houghton Mifflin 1974), your summary sentence (remembering to stretch out a word like **curious**) might be:

George gets in trouble by being too cureus.

Writing a Sentence and Focusing on Finger Spacing between Words

If students are not using spaces between words (they should if you model and talk about this during the morning message), then during a mini-lesson, focus on a finger space between words. Draw a picture of two "stick figure" sisters and write:

These are my sisters Laura and Melissa.

Focus not only on writing the sentence, but also on the finger space between each of the words. "I begin my sentence with a capital letter, and I write the first word 'These.' I leave a finger space before the next word, and then I write 'are.'"

Mini-Lesson Focus: Modeling How to Write Two Sentences

Once most children are writing a sentence you can begin to write two sentences about the same topic in your mini-lesson. Some teachers move quickly from one sentence to two sentences. What you do and when you do it depends on the children in your class.

The teacher starts with a simple sentence and then adds another sentence to it:

"I love my cat. His name is Butch Kitty."

I love my cat.

His name is Butch Kitty.

The teacher may say more but does not write it. "He likes to watch birds in the birdbath. I wonder what he would do if he were an outside cat."

The teacher talks about how she can tell more than just, "I love my cat."

"I can tell his name. I can tell about the things he does. I can tell what he likes to eat or where he likes to sleep."

The teacher lets each student write one sentence and then add another.

While they are writing, she walks around the room and encourages them by asking questions. "What is your cat's (dog's) name? What do you do with your friend? What did you do with your grandma or grandpa?"

After children write, she gathers the students in a circle and lets them share their pictures and sentences.

Others Ideas for Modeling How to Write Two Sentences

Talking and Writing about Your Favorite College or Professional Sports Team or a Local Team

Most children are aware of professional, college or university, or even the local high school football or basketball team, especially if the teams are playing well. They may watch the teams on television or in person. Share your experiences with them, and they will share their experiences with you! Talk about going to the basketball game, tell them who you cheered for, and then write about it.

Wake Forest beat North Carolina last night!
My sister and I cheered and cheered.

It is all right to be honest. Not all children like sports, but some do. Write about a wide range of topics to stir an interest in the many children in your class.

Writing about Things You Don't Like and Things You Do Like

My husband likes football.
I like the halftime show.

Talking and Writing about Places You Go and How You Like Them

If you write about topics some students have never heard of, you expand their vocabularies and knowledge. Tell the children what an opera is and all about the story and the singing. Then, write:

I went to the opera on Sunday.
It was a beautiful love story.

Writing about Things You Do with Your Family and Friends

The children will get to know you, your family, and your friends. You will become a "real" person, not just their teacher. But, even more importantly, they will see that life is full of stories to tell.

Ann and I went to lunch on Sunday.
It was cold so we ordered soup.

Talking and Writing about Special Days, Events, or Happenings at School

Children like to know the things you do. They may also be able to share some of the same experiences.

Yesterday, I bought valentine cards.
Some are pretty and some are funny.

or

Yesterday, it snowed.
We did not have school.

Mini-Lesson Focus: Expanding One Sentence with Questions

When your children are at the point that most of them are capable of daily writing at least one good sentence each (and many are writing two sentences each), then they are ready to learn how to add more sentences. Tell the children that once they have one good sentence, thinking of questions will help them think of other sentences.

The teacher thinks aloud and begins to write:

"I am drawing a picture or outline of a car."

"Now, I will write a sentence to go with my picture. I think I'll write:"

This is my new car.

"This sentence tells about my picture, but I have more to tell. What else should I write? What do you want to know about my car?"

The teacher lets children ask her questions about her new car:

"What color is your car?"

"What kind of car is it?"

"Where do you go in your car?"

"Who rides in the car with you?"

The teacher reads the sentence again and then answers the questions as she writes more:

"This is my new car. It is a green Toyota®. I drive it to school. Sometimes, my mother rides with me. I take her to the store."

She encourages each child to write about something (the family car, van, sports utility vehicle, etc.) and tell her all about it.

The teacher circulates around the room as children begin drawing their pictures and writing their first sentences. She asks them questions that help them think of more sentences.

After children write, she gathers them in a circle and lets them share their pictures and sentences.

Other Ideas for Expanding One Sentence with Questions

Writing One Sentence that Elicits Questions from Students

Write one sentence as you say it to the class.

I went to the mall.

Put down your pen (pencil or marker) and say you are done! The usual response is for children to ask questions like: "Who did you go with? When did you go there? What stores did you go to at the mall? What did you buy?" Answer these questions and add to your story.

I went to the mall. I went with my friend Elaine. We went after school. We went in lots of stores. I bought a new pair of shoes.

Showing a Picture and Writing a Sentence about It

Find a picture in a magazine, a tour book, or an old calendar of a place that you know some of your children have visited. Talk about the picture and write a sentence.

Tanglewood Park is a nice place to visit.

Ask the children questions about the picture and your sentence: "Where is it? Who has gone to Tanglewood? Who did you go with? Why did you go there? When did you go? What did you do there?" Have different children answer these questions and use the answers to add to your writing. The completed piece might look like this:

Tanglewood Park is near our school. Many children go there with their families. In the summer, they swim in the pool. In December, there is a beautiful light show there. Our class will go there for a picnic at the end of the year.

Showing a Picture and Using the Five "W" questions

Depending on your class, you may be able to talk about the five "W" questions (Who, What, Where, When, and Why). Show a picture of someone and write:

This is Christine Murphy.

Show the five "W" questions to your class—they may be on a chart or glove (one question on each finger). Answer each question with a complete sentence and write these sentences after the first sentence.

This is Christine Murphy. She is my sister. She lives in California and does "The Murphy Report" for her local television station. Every summer, Chrissy flies to Rhode Island and North Carolina with her daughter, Zannie, to visit me.

Mini-Lesson Focus: Writing Is Telling about Something

Many children like to write about what is alive, vital, and real for them. Other children listen and learn that they can also write. As teachers, you have to get that message to **all** children. Writing is simply telling about things that are important in our lives. Writing is simply telling things on paper! Everyone can do it.

The teacher thinks aloud:

"What can I write about today? Let's see. What do I know a lot about? I know about things that have happened to me. What has happened to me lately? Has anything interesting happened to anyone I know? I know! My neighbor got a new bike last night. I remember when I was young and got my first bike! I was six years old when I got it. It was so scary learning to ride a two-wheeler!

The teacher tells:

"When I was six years old I got a two-wheeler for my birthday. I was so excited. But I did not know how to ride this bike. I had only been on a bike once. It was my friend Beverly's bike. It was a little bike but it was a two-wheeler. I was very little, but I could put my feet down on the ground, so I was not scared. But when I got my first bike it was red and it was big. When I sat on it I could touch the pedals, but my feet could hardly touch the ground. The wheels just kept wobbling as I tried to pedal it. I was afraid I might fall. I was afraid that I could not keep that bike up straight or stop it if I wanted to stop. Every day after school I practiced riding my bike. Every day I got a little better. Soon I could ride like an expert. I was no longer scared. I have liked riding a bike ever since."

The teacher writes:

When I was six, I got my first bike. When I tried to ride my bike it wobbled. I was scared. I rode it every day until I got good. I still like riding my bike!

The teacher and the children read the writing together:

The teacher reads what she has written with the children and asks: "Can you see a picture of the story in your mind? This is a true story about something that happened in my life. Because I remember it, I can tell you about it and write about it. That's what writing is all about—telling things. Sometimes, we tell true stories, like learning to ride a bike, and sometimes we use our imaginations to make up stories." She reminds the children that the easiest and best way to write a good story is simply to tell a story from their lives. "All of us hear stories from our parents, our brothers and sisters, our neighbors, and our friends. When we write, we are just telling these stories on paper!"

Other Ideas for Writing Is Telling about Something

Reading Stories from the Lives of Other Children

Read a story written by a student from a previous year; choose a story that clearly came from the child's own life. (Many teachers make copies of pieces they know they want to use in future lessons.) Ask where the writer got the idea for the story. Children usually quickly understand that these are events that really happened in the life of the writer.

Next, ask children why they think the writer chose that specific time to write about. They will usually answer that it was a special time, or a time that was really important to the writer for one reason or another. It might have been a time when the writer had strong emotions. The writer may have been very excited, scared, happy, or sad.

Finally, ask students why they think the writer remembered so many details about this time in her life. Help children understand that when something makes you have strong emotions or feelings, you don't even have to try to remember it. It's in your mind and heart to stay. That's why telling a story from your life is the easiest way to write, because all of the details and events are already in your mind.

Finding the Stories in Your Life

Make a list of five things from your own life that would make good stories to tell. Read this list with your children and pick one of them to write about today.

My good friend, Pat

My new bathroom (kitchen, car, etc.)

Planting a flower garden

My daughters (son, cat, dog, husband, best friend, etc.)

My trip to the beach (mountains, lake, coast, etc.)

Helping Children Find Their Stories

Have children brainstorm events that have happened to them that they will probably never forget. Make a list with some children's names and their ideas.

Jake-getting my new video game

Tess-being a cheerleader

Sam-catching a fish with Grandpa

Ideas from Books Read Aloud

Remind children of a book you have recently read aloud to them, such as *Ira Sleeps Over* by Bernard Waber (Houghton Mifflin, 1987). Ask them where they think the author got the idea for this book. Write a few sentences about something in the book you, or someone you know, have experienced.

My nephew, John, had a sleepover for his birthday. . . .

Mini-Lesson Focus: What to Do about Spelling

What to do about spelling is always a concern among teachers who are teaching young children to write. Just how many words can we really expect five-year-olds to spell correctly? In Building-Blocks classrooms, teachers encourage young writers to spell words the best they can by stretching them out. They model stretching out words and then put down the letters they hear. This is helpful once children have letter-sound correspondence. Building-Blocks teachers also teach children how to use the print in the room—names, color words, number words, days, months, weather words, etc. Kindergarten classrooms usually have a wealth of print on the walls. From the very beginning of your writing time, encourage children to "read the room." But when they can't find an unknown word in the room, they should stretch it out and write the letter sounds they hear.

The teacher thinks aloud about what to write:

"In a few weeks, we will have our spring break. Today, I am going to write about what I will do that week."

The teacher writes and talks about how words are spelled:

In April we have our spring brak. ("**April** is on the calendar." She looks at the calendar as she writes April. "**We** is on the morning message, so I can just look over there to spell we. **Spring** is over there on the bulletin board, 'All about Spring.'" The teacher stretches out **break** ("br-ak"), pausing between the beginning letter sound and the rest of the word. She writes the letters as she says the sounds. I will (glances at the morning message again) vizit (stretches out **visit** and writes "vizit") my sister Kathy. ("We have a student named **Kathy** in our room so I can look over at the children's names in our class and see Kathy.") She lives in Sedona. ("If I can spell **we**, I can change the beginning letters and write **she**.") Sedona ("I wrote **Sedona** before; let me copy it.") has rocks of all colors. ("The word **colors** is on the wall.") Sedona is ("We all know how to write **is**.") butiful! (stretches out **beautiful** and writes "butiful")

The teacher reminds children that in their writing today, they should use the words in the room to help them spell words that are found on the walls and stretch out other words that they cannot spell or find on the walls.

Other Ideas for What to Do about Spelling

Teaching Students How to "Read the Room"

Most kindergarten classrooms have color words, number words, days of the week, and months of the year up on the walls. (If you don't, stop right now and post them.) Every kindergarten classroom needs to be a print-rich environment so children can "read the room." Teachers can also label things in their classrooms. Label the clock, the calendar, the easel, the blackboard, etc. Show children how to "read the room" and model this in your writing mini-lessons. The children will be able to spell a lot of words just by looking at the print in your classroom. Don't assume that all children will do this automatically. Many children not only have to be told but also shown how to do this. For some children you will have to model this over and over throughout the year and remind them of this during writing conferences.

- When writing about vehicles, you can model how to use the color words in the room.

    My car is green. ("**Green** is on the color chart.") My mom's car is blue. ("**Blue** is on the color chart.") My sister's car is white. ("**White** is on the color chart.") My bike is red. ("**Red** is on the color chart, too.")

- When writing about classroom activities, you can model how to use the calendar.

    On Monday, ("I can spell **Monday** by looking at the calendar.") we go to music. On Tuesday, ("The calendar helps me spell all the days and months.") we go to the media center.

Teaching Children to Use Bulletin Boards and Theme Boards to Spell Words

Most kindergarten classrooms have bulletin boards with pictures to go with the unit or theme being studied. Add topic-related words to those boards and you have another spelling resource readily available to your children.

"Today, I am going to write about our science topic, weather. I bet I will need a lot of words from our 'Weather' bulletin board."

The weather ("**Weather** is the title word on the board.") is changing. The days are warm. ("**Warm** is one of our weather words.")

Starting a Chart of Month-Related Words Each Month

Post a chart with the name of the month. Have children brainstorm words related to that month. Write these words and add the children's ideas to the chart as the month continues. Refer to this chart as you write during your mini-lessons this month.

Using the Rubber Band/Bubble Gum Analogy to Help Students Learn to Stretch Out Words

To help children understand what stretching out words means, you might want to use a rubber band and stretch it as you stretch out some of the words in your mini-lesson. Tell the children that stretching their words is like stretching a rubber band or bubble gum. They stretch words out and listen for the sounds they hear.

In Building-Blocks classrooms, provide lots of in-room print support for spelling and teach children how to use that support and how to stretch out words. However, DO NOT spell words for children!

Mini-Lesson Focus: Modeling How to Write Using Think-Alouds

Modeling how to write using "think-alouds" is one of the best ways to get kindergarten children to write. Kindergartners like to do what the teacher does. If you model something, they will try it! Think-alouds can be used to model any part of writing that you want to teach! Use think-alouds to model choosing a topic, referring to the classroom to find words, stretching out words, writing more about a topic, etc. Anything that helps children write can and should be modeled using think-alouds.

The teacher says:

"What should I write about today? Should I write about my family, Wake Forest University (where I went to college), my cat, my birthday? I think I will write about my birthday. Did you know I had a birthday over the weekend?"

The teacher thinks aloud and writes:

"I begin my sentence with a capital letter." (The teacher does each thing as she says it.)

Saturday was my birthday.

"I put a capital at the beginning of **Saturday**, because the names of days begin with capitals. I know how to spell Saturday because it is on our calendar . . . was, w-a-s, my, m-y, birthday. Where do you see **birthday** in our room? Yes, it is under the birthday balloons. I end my sentence with a period because telling sentences always end that way."

I went to dinr at Leons.

"I begin this sentence with a capital I, went, w-e-n-t, to . . . I know how to spell **to**; it is one of those 'popcorn' words that keep popping up in our morning messages and when reading big books. **Dinner** is a hard word for kindergartners to spell and when a word is hard to spell, you can stretch it out and write the sounds you hear. (She stretches out and writes "din," then pauses and stretches out and writes "r".) **At** is another 'popcorn' word . . . a-t . . . Leons (stretches out "Le-ons"). I end my sentence with a period."

It snod.

"**It** is one of those 'popcorn' words I know how to spell because it keeps popping up in our reading and writing. **Snowed**—I need to stretch that out and listen . . . "sn-o-d." Once again, I end my sentence with a period."

The teacher thinks aloud and talks about using capital letters and periods. Not all children are ready for this, but the ones who are will pick up this information and use it. The teacher also uses this opportunity to stretch out a word or two so that the children will know how to stretch out and spell words they are not familiar with. She shows kindergartners how to use the print in the room to spell words. Because she thinks aloud as she writes each day, more and more children will come to understand and use the processes she models and talks about.

When sharing a student's writing the teacher asks, "What did you have to think about as you were writing today?"

Other Ideas for Modeling How to Write Using Think-Alouds

In some mini-lessons, you want to focus on one particular part of the writing process. Here are some think-aloud examples focusing on periods and beginning capitals, capital letters for names and I, and choosing topics.

Teaching Ending Punctuation and Beginning Capitals

Write a short piece and only think aloud about your use of capital letters and periods. Toward the end of your lesson, stop and ask children what you should put at the end of your sentence and what kind of letter you need to begin the next sentence.

"Today I am going to write about the Wake Forest University basketball team. I will begin my first sentence with a capital **I**."

I went to the basketball game last night.

"I end my first sentence with a period and begin my next sentence with a capital letter."

It was on television. Did you watch the game?

(Toward the end, ask children what you should write: "This is the end of my sentence. What do I need to put here? What kind of letter should I use to start my next sentence?")

Teaching Capital Letters for Names and I

Write a short piece and only think aloud about how you capitalize names and I. Toward the end of your lesson, stop and ask children what kind of letter you should use to begin names and I.

"This weekend I went to a basketball game. I saw lots of you there. Today, I am going to write about who I saw and what they were doing."

I ("**I** is always a capital letter when it is a word.") went to the Wake Forest ("We always use a capital letter at the beginning of names, even names of basketball teams.") basketball game. They played Duke. ("I start with a capital letter at the beginning of **Duke**, because it is another name.") I ("I always use a capital letter when **I** is a word.") saw Hannah and her brother, Will, there. ("I start **Hannah** and **Will** with capital letters because they are names, too.")

Continue writing and commenting on capitals for names and I. Toward the end, ask children what kind of letter to use before writing it.

Using Think-Alouds to Help You Choose Topics

"What should I write about today? Should I write about my family, my dog, my trip to the mall? I think I will write about my friend, Sally. Did you know I have a friend named Sally who is almost ten years old?"

On Saturday, Sally will be ten. She will have a party. Lots of people are coming. I will give her a book and a toy horse. We will have fun!

Mini-Lesson Focus: Deciding What to Write About (Brainstorming)

For many children, writing is easy once they decide what they want to write about. In Building-Blocks classrooms, teachers want children to view writing as telling. They stress that when children write, they write about what they want to tell. During mini-lessons, teachers often think aloud about what they might want to "tell today." As the children listen in on the teacher's thinking, they see how she decides what she wants to tell, and they get some ideas about what they might tell.

The teacher thinks aloud:

"Let's see. What do I want to tell you about today? I could tell you about the big wind storm we had on Sunday and how a big tree in my backyard fell down. I could tell you about the movie I went to Friday night. I know. I was cleaning out a closet this weekend and I found some of my favorite books from long ago when I was about your age. I think I will tell you about the books I found."

The teacher writes:

Mrs. Hall's Favorite Books:

1. Curious George

2. The Three Little Pigs

3. Three Billy Goats Gruff

4. Dr. Seuss's ABC

5. The Story of Delicia*

As the teacher writes, the children and teacher talk a little about each book. Many of the children comment that these are some of their favorites, too. Many of the children are not familiar with *Delicia*. The teacher tells the children that this is a book about a doll. The book has real pictures of dolls in it. She wonders aloud if she is the only one with this book today; it is an old book. She promises that she will bring in these books tomorrow and read them to the children.

As the children begin their writing, the teacher notices that some of them are making lists of their favorite books. Part of the purpose of every writing mini-lesson is to help children see that there are many different things you can write about and many different ways to write. Teachers communicate to children that writing is primarily to put down on paper something they want to tell. Sometimes what they want to tell will be on the same topic or in the same form as what the teacher wants to tell. Of course, their writing will always be a little different because it will be their ideas—not the teacher's.

* *The Story of Delicia* was written by Gertrude Newman and published in 1935 by Rand McNally and Company. Someone gave it to me as a child and I still have it.—Dorothy Hall

Other Ideas for Deciding What to Write About

Thinking Aloud about a Few Topics You Don't Write About

On at least a couple of days each week, begin your writing mini-lesson by thinking aloud about a few topics that you don't write about but that may spur the thinking of some of your children. If you say that you could write about meeting Jamie in the grocery store and how cute her baby sister is, Jamie may very well be reminded of the meeting and realize that this would be something she would like to tell about. If you say that you could write about how the gerbil got out of his cage yesterday just before the end of school, some of the children who were involved in the hunt to find him will be reminded of that incident. These children might be inspired to write about it. Thinking aloud about a few topics is a subtle way of planting ideas in the minds of children. Children write best when they are writing about something they know and care about. Teachers don't tell them what they should write about, but they do plant some seeds!

Getting Ideas From Sharing

In kindergarten, teachers often gather the children in a circle after writing and informally ask them, "Who wants to tell us what you were writing about today?" Children hold up their writing and drawing and tell the teacher and class about it—often telling more than they have actually written. This encourages children to see the writing time as telling and allows all of them to feel successful as they share their ideas and experiences. This sharing process in itself gives students ideas for writing as they hear what others have written about. You can make this "getting ideas from others" more explicit by doing an occasional mini-lesson in which you add to a class chart of "Things to Write About." Begin your chart by remembering some of the great ideas people have shared in the last week. Every few weeks, use your mini-lesson time to add to the chart.

Things to Write About

the pet store	favorite books
places we go	the substitute teacher
cousins	riding bikes
baby sisters and brothers	video games
big sisters and brothers	playing games

Getting Ideas from Books

Remind children of a book you read aloud to them or a book the class read. Write about that book or an idea triggered by that book. For example, after reading *The Mitten* by Jan Brett (Putnam Publishing Group, 1996), talk about who or what could go into a lost hat or boot, then write about it.

Getting Ideas from School

Be sure to write about what you are learning in math, or the themes you are studying. Do you have a new student? Do you have a new computer? Are there new activities in the centers?

Mini-Lesson Focus: Adding On to a Piece of Writing

Children need to learn how to add on to a piece of writing. As with everything teachers teach students about writing, the most effective way to teach adding on is to model it. Begin by writing a story one day—thinking aloud, talking, and writing. The next day, model how you can revisit what you wrote, read it over, and add on to it. Taking two or three days to write about the same topic gives children permission to do this. Your most avid writers always have more to say than they can write in one day. Your struggling writers need more than a day if they are ever going to finish their pieces! Encouraging each child to take as many days as he needs to write a piece is one way to make your writing block multilevel—something that works for everyone. Don't worry if some students are still driting as long as they are making progress. Continue to "ooh" and "aah" about what they do.

The first day the teacher thinks aloud about the field trip and writes, modeling how to stretch out some words:

Our Field Trip

Yesterday, our class went to Old Salem. We rode a bus there. Mrs. Daniel and Mrs. Reckord went with us. We vizited the bakery, the church, and a muzeum.

The next day, the teacher wants to add on.

She revisits the piece by thinking aloud, talking about, and rereading what she wrote. She takes out the transparency of (or turns her chart tablet to) the previous day's writing. "Now let's see . . . I started this yesterday. It was all about our field trip to Old Salem. I wrote about how we got there, who went with us, and the buildings we visited. Let's read it together." The teacher reads her writing with the children.

Then, the teacher asks, "Did I tell everything we did? No, I have lots more to tell. I could tell what we saw at the bakery, what we saw in the church, and what we saw at the museum. I could tell about the candlelight tea we went to. Today, I am going to add on to my piece about our field trip." Then, the teacher thinks aloud once again and adds on to the piece, continuing to stretch out a word or two.

In the bakery, we saw people making sugar cake. The church was decorated with canduls. In the muzeum, we saw the tools people used long ago.

To finish this piece, the teacher wants and needs a third day.

She still has not written about the candlelight tea, although she mentioned the church on the second day. She wants to reread her writing from the first two days and finishes her piece on a third day.

We went to a candullight tea in the church. We all got a small candul to take home. We got a Moravian bun to eat and something to drink. We had fun!

After writing each day, the teacher dismisses the children by task: "Those who are still writing on a piece in their journal can go back to their seats and finish writing now. Those who want to start a new piece of writing can go back to their seats."

Other Ideas for Adding On to a Piece of Writing

Writing about Something that Happened to You and Stopping before the Ending

Think aloud and begin to write your story:

> Yesterday was a terrible, horrible day. First, I overslept. I had to hurry and I missed my breakfast. I got to school late.

The next day, reread your writing, then ask, "When I stopped yesterday, I had started writing about my morning. Do you think I am finished with my story?" Continue to write:

> I missed a meeting. Then, it rained, and we could not go outside to play. After school, I found my car had a flat tire. It was a bad day all day long!

Writing a Class Summary about a Story You Have Read in Guided Reading

Begin a summary of a story your class read during the shared reading of a big book. The example below uses *Mrs. Wishy-Washy* by Joy Cowley (Philomel Books, 1999). Write the beginning one day.

> This story begins with all of the animals getting dirty. The cow, pig, and duck like rolling in the mud.

Add the middle the next day.

> When Mrs. Wishy-Washy sees the dirty animals, she says, "In the tub you go!" In they went, and she scrubs them, wishy-washy, wishy-washy.

The end can be written on the third day.

> But when the animals saw the mud again, they got dirty again! What will Mrs. Wishy-Washy do now?

Sharing a Student's Writing and Helping Him Revisit the Piece and Add On

Make a transparency of a child's story that could have something added on. Read the story together as a class. Then, as a class, add on to the story and finish it together!

Finishing a Story Started in the Teacher Read-Aloud

After reading the beginning of a book that is too long to finish in one teacher read-aloud, write a summary of the story so far. The next day, revisit your summary and write the ending of the story. Ask students what they think will happen. Think aloud and write their ending. Compare your writing—how you ended the story—to the author's ending after you finish reading the book. You will find that sometimes, kindergarten children (and their teachers) can think of endings just as good or better than the author, and sometimes it is hard to better the original!

Mini-Lesson Focus: Choosing a Title for Your Writing

In Building-Blocks classrooms, teachers want children to view writing as telling. Teachers stress that when people write, they write about what they want to tell. As children begin to write, they often put a name or title on their writing. A child wants to tell about her baby doll and she writes, "My Baby," at the top of her paper. It's time to talk about titles, and how to choose them, and when.

The teacher thinks aloud:

"Let's see. What do I want to tell you about today? I could tell you about the new book I just bought. I think I will save that to read to you later today. I could tell you about the basketball game I went to at the coliseum on Saturday. My team lost so I don't think that would be fun to write about. I know. I will tell you about the cookies I baked last night. I baked enough of them to bring one for everyone in our class and still have enough for my family!"

The teacher thinks aloud and writes:

"Since this is going to be about cookies, I will write that first as my title." Then, she writes, Baking Cookies at the top of her transparency (or chart paper) to begin her writing.

Next, she thinks aloud about what she did, why she did it, and how to write it. "I like to bake cookies for my family and friends. Buying cookies is easy, but baking cookies is fun. You need to collect all of the ingredients before you begin. You need the recipe and you need to follow the directions. The best thing about baking cookies is eating them!" She then talks and writes:

Yesterday, I made chocolate chip cookies. First, I found the ingredence. ("I stretch out that word as I spell it like it sounds.") Then, I mixed all the ingredence in a big bowl. I dropped the cookies by spoonfuls on the baking sheet. After I baked them, I took some to my students at school and saved some for my children at home.

The teacher and the class read the story and talk about the title.

"I wrote the name or the title first. Sometimes you know what you will write about and put that on your paper at the beginning. At other times you have an idea, but are not sure what a good title will be. You can wait until after you have finished writing and see exactly what you have written, then come up with a title. After you finish your writing, it is always a good idea to reread what you wrote and say to yourself, is this a good title for my writing? Let's do that now."

"'Baking Cookies' is one name for this piece. What else could I have named this?" The children give her these titles: "Chocolate Chip Cookies," "Cookies for My Family and Friends," and "Baking Cookies Is Fun." The teacher knows that the class can vote on the best title or she can decide which title she thinks is best. She decides another name is better than her original, so she changes the title to "Baking Cookies Is Fun."

In kindergarten, titles are usually decided one-on-one during coached writing conferences teachers have with students. Most kindergarten children have enough to do just to write. But talking about titles is appropriate for other children as they begin to publish.

Other Ideas for Choosing a Title for Your Writing

Writing and Having Students Think of Titles

Write about something you have done and have the children come up with 3-4 possible titles. Choose or vote on which is the best. Put that title at the top of your paper. You could write about going to a basketball game to see Wake Forest University play against the University of North Carolina and Wake Forest winning (choose your favorite team or a local team). The children give you these possible titles: "Wake Forest Wins;" "Wake Forest Beats North Carolina;" and "Watching a Great Game." All of the titles are good, so you let the children vote to decide. They choose "Wake Forest Wins." You write that at the top of the piece.

Choosing a Title and Writing, Then Deciding that the Title Needs to Be Changed

Choose the title, "My Cat" (or use any animal that is a pet). Write about your pet cat (or someone in the room's pet).

My cat, Butch Kitty, likes to sleep in the sun. He sleeps on the windowsill. He sleeps on the floor where the sun shines. Where there is sun, there is Butch Kitty sleeping.

Decide that this story is not all about your cat, but about something your cat likes to do—he likes to sleep in the sun. With your class, brainstorm some different titles: "My Cat Sleeps in the Sun;" "A Sun Sleeper;" "Butch Kitty Sleeps;" etc. Choose the one you (or the class) like best. If it is "My Cat Sleeps in the Sun," then draw a line through the old title and write the new one above it.

Choosing a Title for an Informational Piece You Write

Teachers often work with "stories" to choose a title. You need to do this for informational pieces also. Write the title "Plants" (or "Planting Seeds") and have the children write what they know on this topic.

Choosing a Title for an Informational Piece and Writing, Then Deciding that the Title Needs to Be Changed

Write the title "Spring." Write about animals having babies in spring. Decide that this is about animal babies and not just spring. With your class, brainstorm new titles for this piece. Choose one you or your class likes best. Draw a line through the old title and write the new title "Spring Babies."

Mini-Lesson Focus: Coached Writing and Procedures for Publishing

Example #1

By now your kindergarten students are in the habit of writing each day, and they have learned to "add on" to a piece and can spend several days writing a piece. At this point, you are ready for the part of Writer's Workshop that parents absolutely love—publishing! Publishing, which really means making writing public, gives children a finished product. In kindergarten, we do not expect perfect published pieces like we do in first grade and up. Most teachers find it easier and more manageable if the children begin to publish at different times and if the goal is one book per child by the end of the year.

The first coached writing session for one little girl:

Ginna wrote a piece titled "My Sister and Me." At the first coached writing session, she wrote, "I like my sester. We play togater." Ginna knew the high-frequency words: **my**, **me**, **we**, and **play** and was able to use these words in her writing. She also knew how to sound out the words **sister** ("sester") and **together** ("togater"). Ginna is aware that her story is not done; she needs at least five sentences on the topic, and she has two when she is asked to count her sentences. She adds, "We colr and we have rases. We camp togater. We like to play ball togater." These five sentences complete her first coached writing session.

The second coached writing session for the same child:

Ginna reads the "story" she has written so far. She continues to give details about her life with her sister and tell about all of the things they like to do together. She adds, "We shar toys and we shar clos. We pec flwrs for mom and we help set the tabl." Then, she adds, "We play band, skat, and read books togater." She is aware of how to spell the high-frequency words: **we**, **and**, **for**, **play**, and **the**. She also knows the spelling of **read**, **mom**, **help**, **set**, and **book**, recognizing those words from print in the classroom. She stretches out and sound-spells **share** ("shar"), **close** ("clos"), **pick** ("pec"), **flowers** ("flawrs"), **table** ("tabl"), **skate** ("skat"), and **together** ("togater"). She decides to end her story in a special way, "A sester is fun and I love my sester." It takes Ginna two sessions of coached writing to complete a story for publishing.

After the book is put together, the student illustrates the pages in her book.

If Ginna had handwritten this piece, then someone (teacher, assistant, or parent helper) would have to type it on the computer and print the page. Because Ginna has been coached on a computer, her "story" just needs to be printed, the sentences cut apart, pasted on pages, and illustrated.

When finished the teacher writes the "All about the Author" page.

The teacher asks Ginna to tell about herself and writes a page about the author—Ginna.

Ginna is in kindergarten. She likes to write in school. She likes to play with her sister at home. She likes pizza and ice cream. She will be a teacher when she grows up.

My Sister and Me
by
Ginna

I like my sester. We play togater.

We color and we have rases.

We camp togater. We like to play ball togater.

We shar toys and we shar clos. We pec flawrs for mom and we help set the tabl.

We play band, skat, and read books togater.

A sester is fun and I love my sester.

Ginna is in kindergarten. She likes to write in school. She likes to play with her sister at home. She likes pizza and ice cream. She will be a teacher when she grows up.

Mini-Lesson Focus: Coached Writing and Procedures for Publishing

Example #2

Kindergarten students are ready to publish a piece when they can write with phonics spelling, know letter sounds, and how to form letters. For some children, it is easier to compose on the computer so they do not have to worry about handwriting. Some children do better writing on the computer if you use a larger font than usual.

The first coached writing session for one boy:

Robbie writes a piece about T-Ball. At the first coached writing session he writes, " I play te bol." Then, he writes, "I like te-bol." Robbie knows the high-frequency words **I**, **play**, and **like**, and he is able to use them in his writing. He also knows how to sound out the word **T-ball** ("te-bol"). Then, Robbie asks, "Do you know why I like T-ball?" The teacher tells him that would be a good sentence to write next. So Robbie begins to say and write each word in the sentence. He writes, "Do (He begins his sentence with a capital letter.) you no ("no" is what he hears for **know** and what he writes) wi ("wi" is what he hears for **why** and what he writes) I like it?"

The teacher asks, "Can you answer that question?" Robbie answers, "I can catch the ball. I can hit the ball. It is fun." Robbie begins to say each word and writes the words he says: "I (a high-frequency word he can spell) can (another high-frequency word he can spell) caj (he stretches out the word **catch** and writes the sounds he hears) the (a high-frequency word he can spell) bol (he stretches out the word **ball** and spells it just as he has done before). I can (two high-frequency words he can spell) het (stretches out the word **hit** and spells it as best he can) the (a high-frequency word he can spell) bol (stretches out **ball** and spells it as he has done before). It is fun (three high-frequency words he can spell)."

Robbie has the required number of sentences, but when the teacher asks if his writing is finished he says, "No!" These seven sentences complete his first coached writing session, but he wants to add more, so the teacher plans to work with him again tomorrow.

The second coached writing session for the same child:

With help from his teacher, Robbie reads the "story" he has written so far. He decides to finish it by adding, "I can get a home run. It is fun and I like it." Robbie is aware of how to spell the high-frequency words (**I**, **can**, **get**, **a**, and **run**), but he has to stretch out **home** ("hom"). He also knows the spelling of **it**, **is**, **fun**, **and**, **I**, **like**, and **it** in the second sentence. His final sentence is, "I caught a ball and I was happy." We writes **I**, **a**, and **happy** from memory and stretches out **caught** and writes "cait." He stretches out **was** and writes "wuz." Robbie decides that is a good ending and is pleased with his "story" about playing T-ball.

On the third day, the piece is reread and printed.

The sentences are cut apart and pasted on separate sheets of paper. Then, the teacher and Robbie talk about how to illustrate the pages in the book.

When they are finished, the teacher writes the "All about the Author" page.

Robbie lives in Clemmons and likes to draw pictures. He likes to play with his brother. He likes to play T-ball! He wants to be a fireman when he grows up.

T-Ball
by
Robbie

I play te bol.

I like te bol.
Do you no wi I like it?

I can caj the bol. I can het the bol. It is fun.

I can get a hom run. It is fun and I like it.

I cait a bol and I wuz happy.

Robbie lives in Clemmons and likes to draw pictures. He likes to play with his brother. He likes to play T-ball! He wants to be a fireman when he grows up.

Mini-Lesson Focus: Coached Writing and Procedures for Publishing

Example #3

Some kindergarten students use more "phonics spelling" than other children. Allowing them to stretch out words helps them write and then be able to read their "stories" back to you. If you changed these words to conventional spelling, then the students would not be able to read them back. This is the coached writing of one such child.

The first coached writing session for one kindergarten child:

Rani is writing about her birthday. This is a subject Rani knows a lot about, so background knowledge is no problem. Her birthday is also something she is excited to share with her friends, so motivation is not a problem either!

Rani begins her "story" with a smile. "I will have my birthday at Skateland." She writes **I**, **will**, and **at** from memory. She stretches out **have** ("hav"), **birthday** ("brthday"), and **Skateland** ("scatland"). She says her next sentence, "I will have lots of people over." **I** and **will** are high-frequency words she knows. She stretches out and writes the other words: **have** ("hav"), **lots** ("los"), **of** ("ov"), **people** ("pepl"), and **over** ("ovr").

The second coached writing session for the same child:

Rani reads the "story" she has written so far. She can read it well because it is her writing and her "phonics spelling." She decides to finish it by adding, "At Skateland, we will skate and do lots of tricks. I am excited. I like my birthday. I am happy. I am going to be 6. We will have a busy day." She adds the sentences one at a time. She says what she wants to say because she is allowed to stretch out words she does not know and writes them. Rani knows the high-frequency words **at**, **we**, **will**, **and**, **I**, **like**, **my**, **am**, **to**, **be**, **a**, and **day**. She copies **Skateland** ("scatland"), **lots** ("los"), **have** ("hav"), and **birthday** ("brthday") from her other sentences. She stretches out **skate** ("scat"), **do** ("dew"), **of** ("ov"), **tricks** ("trecs"), **excited** ("ecsited"), **happy** ("hape"), **going** ("goy"), and **busy** ("beze").

On the third day, the piece is reread and printed.

The sentences are cut apart and pasted on separate sheets of paper. The teacher and the student then talk about how to illustrate the pages in the book.

When they are finished, the teacher writes the "All about the Author" page.

Rani lives in Clemmons with her sister and 2 cousins. She loves to play in centers and read Cinderella. She likes to eat pizza and play with her sisters. She wants to be a teacher someday! She will be a great one!

My Birthday
by
Rani

I will hav my brthday at scatland.

I will hav los ov pepl ovr.

At scatland we will scat and dew los ov trecs. I am ecsited.

I like my brthday. I am hape. I am goy to be 6.

We will hav a beze day.

Rani lives in Clemmons with her sister and 2 cousins. She loves to play in centers and read Cinderella. She likes to eat pizza and play with her sisters. She wants to be a teacher someday! She will be a great one!

Mini-Lesson Focus: Writing a Story (Beginning, Middle, End)

Remind students that when you read aloud to them, the books are often "stories" with a beginning, middle, and end. Students also need to be reminded that during the shared reading of big books, they talk about the beginning, middle, and end of the story. This mini-lesson is about writing a story with a beginning, middle, and end.

The teacher thinks aloud about what to write:

"I could write a story about visiting my sister who lives in another city. My trip to her house would begin that story. I could write about a ball game I watched. I know how that story would end—with my favorite team winning. I could write about one of my favorite books, *Rainbow Fish* (North South Books, 1992). That story has a good beginning, middle, and end. Since we are talking about the beginning, middle, and end of a story, that is what I will write—a story about my friend, Ann.

The teacher thinks aloud and writes:

Ann

Ann has been my friend for a long time. We were friends when we were your age. We were friends before she got married and had three girls, Eleanor, Susan, and Sally.

She rereads the beginning, then talks about and writes more things she wants to tell (a middle to her story).

Ann and I like to shop. We like to eat lunch together. Sometimes we go to church together. Whatever we do, we have fun.

The teacher rereads the beginning and middle, then talks about and writes the end.

This year, Ann, Eleanor, and I will go to New York City. We will see a Broadway show. We will have fun!

Sometimes you write about special people because you want your students to know what is happening in your life. Children do the same for you when they write. Sometimes young children's stories let you know what is happening in their lives—sometimes it is happy and sometimes it is sad.

Other Ideas for Writing a Story (Beginning, Middle, End)

Writing about Something that Happened to You. Be Sure the Story Has a Beginning, Middle, and End

One thing that teachers write about all of the time is events that happen to them or their children. Choose a familiar topic, think aloud, and write your story with a clear beginning, middle, and end. You will probably need to add on to your piece across several days.

Our Trip to Lake Norman

One Saturday we got up early, packed a lunch, and headed for Lake Norman. We loaded our boat with drinks and lunch. Off we went for a boat ride.

We rode all over the lake. We stopped to swim in the lake. We got back just before it rained. We had fun!

Writing about One of Your Students. Be Sure the Story Has a Beginning, Middle, and End

Have a private conversation with the student before you write about what happened at the beginning, middle, and end. This story allows you to review capitals for names and places.

Shopping with Grandma

Linda likes to go shopping with her Grandma. They go to the farmer's market on Saturday. They get up early. Grandma buys fruits and vegetables. Linda gets to pick out the corn and tomatoes. Sometimes they buy flowers. Then, they come home and show everyone what they bought. Linda likes to shop with Grandma.

Letting the Class Help You Write a Story Based on a Story They All Know and Enjoy

Review a favorite story such as *Sylvester and the Magic Pebble* by William Steig (Aladdin Library, 1987). Talk about the beginning, middle, and end of this story. Let the class help you write the story about this book across several days.

Sylvester lived with his mother and father and was very happy. One day he found a pebble. He made a wish and it came true. It was a magic pebble.

Mini-Lesson Focus: Writing an Informational Piece (Using a Web)

Often when teachers and kindergarten children think about writing they think about writing "stories." When you write about things the class is learning about or things you know a lot about, these are not really "stories." You call them informational pieces. Informational books are not structured in the same way that stories are. Writing informational pieces is different from writing stories.

The teacher thinks aloud about what to write:

"Sometimes I write about things we are studying in kindergarten. Sometimes I write about the things you know a lot about, like cats or dinosaurs. When people write about something and they want to make sure they tell everything they know, they often start with a web. If I choose to write about dinosaurs, a web would help me organize what I know about dinosaurs. Today, since we are studying insects, I am going make a web about insects and then use that web to write what we know about them."

The teacher thinks aloud and starts a web:

"Since I am going to write about insects, I will put the word insects in the middle. What do we know about insects from the books we have read?"

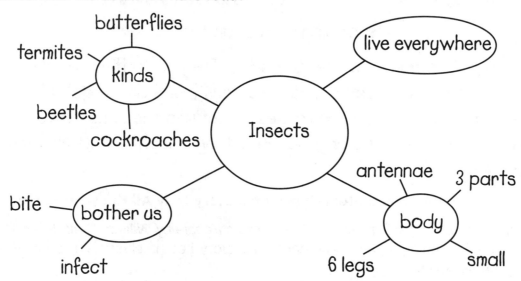

The teacher finishes making the web, then reads and reviews it with the children.

The teacher thinks aloud and begins to write about insects using the web:

Insects

There are many insects. Some insects we know are beetles, termites, butterflies, and cockroaches. They live all over the world. Insects are small. They have 6 legs. They have 3 body parts and antennae. They bother us when they bite us or harm our body, food, or houses. There are lots of books to read and learn about insects.

Other Ideas for Writing an Informational Piece (Using a Web)

Making a Web about Your Family When You Talk about Families

Writing about families is harder than it used to be. Families have changed, and these changes include a variety of "other" people. If your class has many traditional families then write about one of them. If some children are in unique situations, then talk about other kinds of families, too. Perhaps you can let the children tell who is in their families, web two or three responses, and write about those families using a web.

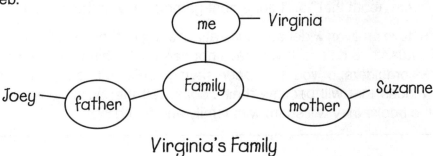

Virginia's Family

Virginia has three people in her family. She has a father named Joey, a mother named Suzanne, and then there is Virginia.

Writing about Friends When You Are Talking about Friends

Students learn all about friends in kindergarten as they make new friends. Talk about what friends are like and what they do. Then, make a web to help you and students write about friends.

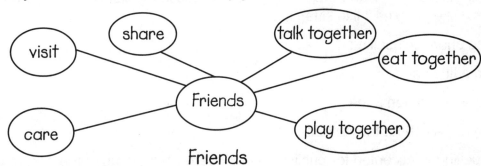

Friends

In school, we have many friends. Friends play together. Friends share their toys and take turns. Friends . . . .

Writing about Things You Are Talking about (the wind, spring, March, etc.), Making a Web, Then Writing from the Web

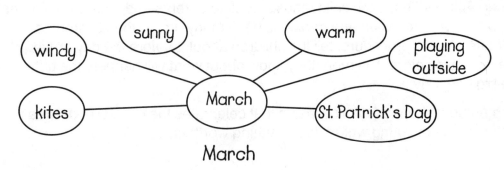

March

March is the start of spring. The days are warm and windy. We see . . . .

Mini-Lesson Focus: Young Authors' Celebration

Now that your kindergarten students have become young authors, it is important to take time to celebrate this feat. Setting aside time for children to share their writing is an important part of the writing process. It also gives students opportunities to develop listening and speaking skills. After writing each day, the children get to share their writing with the other students in a circle or Author's Chair format. This is a time when some children get ideas for stories they can write. ("I have a dog, too. I can write about how my dog is always digging holes in my backyard," or "I went to the park with my grandpa. I can write about that," or "I got a neat game for my birthday. I could tell about that.")

You can let children have an even wider audience at a "Young Authors' Tea." The last month of school is a good time for students to do this. If you have not been publishing, but your students have been writing in notebooks or folders, or you have been saving some writing on computer disks, then you already have the pieces that will become their books. Tell the class about the upcoming Young Authors' Tea and the books they will share with family and friends.

Guidelines for Publishing in Kindergarten

- Writing five sentences about a topic

- Using correct capitalization and punctuation

- Including a beginning, middle, and end for all stories (fiction writing)

- Accepting "All About . . ." and "I Like . . ." pieces ("This is my sister. We play and sing," or "I like hamsters. I like puppies. I like kittens.")

- Accepting phonetic spelling

- Including a title page

- Including a dedication page

- Including an "All about the Author" page

Phonetic spelling is accepted for publishing in kindergarten because the children can usually read their writing when they practice this strategy. When you correct every word, then many kindergarten children do not recognize their writing. Children are encouraged to write what they know about and take risks in spelling words—that is how they grow in their word knowledge. Applaud their spelling efforts instead of editing their mistakes. Coach each child to have a finished product that he is proud of, but, more importantly, one that he can read without much help.

At the Young Authors' Tea, each child reads a book to parents and other invited guests. Following the readings, a tea party (cookies and drinks) is held. Many times, the children serve their parents and guests. Whatever your procedure, tell the children about it before the day arrives. It would not hurt to practice a few days before. The more they know about what will happen, the better young children do when the big day arrives.

The Young Authors' Tea is a joyful occasion that celebrates the children's desires to learn to read and write. A community of young writers is something worth celebrating.

Other Ideas for Young Authors' Celebration

Writing Invitations to the Young Authors' Tea or Conference

Tell students about invitations and have them help you write a class invitation to the "Young Authors' Tea." You may want to type the invitation on your computer if you can project it onto a screen for all to see. Copy the finished invitation on pieces of paper that can be inserted inside cards decorated by the children.

> You are invited to our Young Authors' Tea
>
> Who: Family and Friends
>
> When: May 12, 2003 at 2:00
>
> Where: Room 25, Clemmons Elementary
>
> We hope you can come!

Writing about What Will Happen at the Young Authors' Tea

Talk about that day and what will happen. Children need to know what will happen at their Young Authors' Tea and what they are expected to do. By doing this mini-lesson you will prepare your children for the events.

> The Young Authors' Tea
>
> Friday is a special day. We will read our books to our parents and friends. Then, we will have a tea party. It will be fun!

Writing about How Your Class Will Read Their Books

Think aloud, tell, and write about how your class will read their books.

> We will divide into three groups to read our books. When it is your turn, you will stand and read. Remember to practice reading so you will do a good job. You can clap after each book (or at the end—you, as the teacher, decide!).

Letting Young Authors Share with Other Classes

Some teachers feel that a big celebration is not what they want, but they still want to share their students' writing beyond the classroom. Sharing with the other kindergarten classes in your school is one way to do this. Invite another class to come and hear your students read their books.

Letting Young Authors Share with Older Children

Send students to an upper-grade class to read their writing. For example, work with the fourth-grade teachers and send one third (if there are three classes) of your students, with their books, to each of the classrooms. Older children just "ooh" and "aah" at what the younger children can do.

References

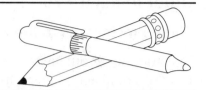

Professional References

Cunningham, P. M. "Beginning Reading Without Readiness: Structured Language Experience" *Reading Horizons* (Spring 1979): 222-227.

Hall, D. P.; Arens, A. B.; and Loman, K. L. (2002) *The Administrator's Guide to Building Blocks™.* Greensboro, NC: Carson-Dellosa Publishing Co.

Hall, D. P. and Cunningham, P. M. (1997) *Month-by-Month Reading and Writing in Kindergarten.* Greensboro, NC: Carson-Dellosa Publishing Co.

Hall, D. P. and Loman, K.L. (2002) *Interactive Charts: Shared Reading for Kindergarten and First Grade.* Greensboro, NC: Carson-Dellosa Publishing Co.

Hall, D. P. and Williams, E. (2001) *Predictable Charts: Shared Writing for Kindergarten and First Grade.* Greensboro, NC: Carson-Dellosa Publishing Co.

Hall, D. P. and Williams, E. (2000) *The Teacher's Guide to Building Blocks™.* Greensboro, NC: Carson-Dellosa Publishing Co.

Children's Books Cited

ABC I Like Me by Nancy Carlson (Viking, 1997)

Curious George by H.A. Rey (Houghton Mifflin, 1973)

Curious George Takes a Job by H.A. Rey (Houghton Mifflin, 1974)

Dr. Seuss's ABC: An Amazing Alphabet Book by Dr. Seuss (Random House, 1996)

Ira Sleeps Over by Bernard Waber (Houghton Mifflin, 1987)

The Mitten by Jan Brett (Putnam Publishing Group, 1996)

Rainbow Fish by Marcus Pfister (North South Books, 1992)

See What I Can Do! by Mary Pearson (Steck-Vaughn Company, 2002)

Sylvester and the Magic Pebble by William Steig (Aladdin Library, 1987)

Mrs. Wishy-Washy by Joy Cowley (Philomel Books, 1999)

Notes

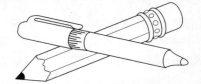

Notes

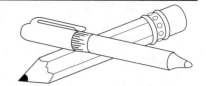